Old BANCHORY

by
David Jamieson & W. Stewart Wilson

HIGH STREET, BANCHORY

The air is full of romance at **BANCHORY**

First published in the United Kingdom, 1999,
by Stenlake Publishing Ltd.
Telephone: 01290 551122

ISBN 1 84033 087 2

ACKNOWLEDGEMENTS

The authors wish to thank many people in Banchory who have helped in the preparation of this book, and in particular Charles Adams, Douglas Black, Charles McIntosh, William Murray, Michael Robson and Dr Alexander S. Waugh.
  The publishers would like to thank Robert Grieves for providing the picture on page 9, and W. A. C. Smith for providing information about the picture on page 8.

The publishers regret that they cannot supply
any copies of pictures featured in this book.

Facing page: The arms of the Burgh of Banchory (1885-1975), granted in 1939, portray Ternan, 'patron saint' of the medieval parish, who is believed to have been the first Christian evangelist on Deeside and the founder of a Christian settlement hereabouts, perhaps in the seventh century. He is shown carrying a book (he is said to have possessed a copy of St Matthew's Gospel bound in gold and silver) and a bell, representing his legendary 'Ronnecht' or songster. The mitre and elaborate pastoral staff (or crozier) are anachronisms representing a medieval bishop or mitred abbot rather than a Celtic holy man of earlier centuries. The holly leaves and the hunting horn come from the arms of the Burnetts of Leys, the builders of Crathes Castle. The eagle comes from the arms of the Ramsays of Balmain in recognition of their kinship with the Burnett Ramsays of Banchory Lodge. The motto, meaning 'Stand Fast', has obvious Gordon connections; there is a fine granite war memorial on the North Deeside Road as you leave Banchory to the west in memory of those of the 7th Battalion of the Gordon Highlanders who lost their lives in the First World War. The arms were a gift to the burgh from Mr James Burnett, who was provost of Banchory from 1928 to 1945.

INTRODUCTION

The development of Banchory – and for that matter Deeside – as a popular place to put down roots or to visit owes a great deal to the selection of Balmoral as a royal residence in the 1840s. In addition, the rainfall of the valley of the Dee reveals it to be one of the driest parts of Scotland, and of course the scenery is magnificent. In the Third Statistical Account of Kincardine the author claims that the number of hours of sunshine on Deeside during the winter months even exceeds that of the south of England!

Over the years Banchory-Ternan has been spelt in a variety of ways. In a document dated 12 June (St Ternan's Day) 1491, the keeper (dewar) of 'the Bell of Saint Ternan' called the 'Ronnecht' renounced his rights in favour of the Vicar of 'Banquhoriterne'. An interesting form of the name, Banchory Trinitie, appears in the accounts of the Collector General for 1562 and 1563. This was also the form used in Blaeu's map of Scotland of 1635 and in a Burnett of Leys family document, dated 10 March 1654.

But back to the beginning of the story. The tradition is that Ternan's settlement was centred on the site of the later (and present-day) kirkyard, which was to become the focus (the Kirkton) of the medieval Parish of Banchory-Ternan. Further, Ternan as a Pict would have spoken a language more closely related to Welsh and Cornish than to Gaelic, which did not arrive on Deeside until the ninth century. Thus the name Banchory corresponds to the Welsh and Cornish Bangors (with such earlier spellings as Bancor and Banchor) and shares the same original meaning of a Christian settlement within a 'wattled or plaited enclosure'. The Bangor in Northern Ireland is believed to have been a daughter foundation of Bangor in Cornwall.

In a charter of 1323/24 the Kirkton of Banchory Ternan is referred to as a village. It was fairly considerable for the time with schools, a church and manse, a hospital, an inn for travellers, and several labourers' cottages.

It was as Kirkton of Leys that the village became a burgh of barony, its charter being dated 25 April 1488. The importance of the Kirkton was partly derived from its proximity to a crossing point over the Dee at the cobleheugh (ferry-bank), with the Cobleheugh Inn being rebuilt as Banchory Lodge in the early nineteenth century. In the late 1700s Kirkton spread eastwards and up the hill, probably partly in response to erosion of the riverbank. This new development was often referred to as Townhead or Townheid. With the building of the bridge over the Dee in 1798 and the construction of the turnpike road in 1802, a new village, known as Arbeadie but often referred to by locals as New Banchory, grew up north-west of Townhead.

Banchory as we know it today owes its development to three men of enterprise and energy. In 1805 William Shaw was granted land at 2/6 per acre by the laird of Tilquhillie; the second feuar in 1807 was John Watson who paid 3/- per acre for his feus; in 1809 William Ewan had to pay 20/- per acre. These men developed the village to the west of New Banchory. The old Kirkton finally had to make way for the arrival of the railway in Banchory in 1853 and the building of Banchory Station.

Banchory soon developed into a very popular place for visitors. In Alex McConnachie's *Deeside*, published in 1900, the author refers to it as 'a summer resort for Aberdonians and tourists which takes precedence, for numbers, over all others, while on holidays excursionists visit it literally in thousands. The Hill of Fare protects Banchory from the cold winds of the north and its southern exposure also contributes to its advantages as a health and holiday resort. Unquestionably nature has done a great deal for Banchory; the marvel is that the century had begun before the nucleus of a town had been founded in such a delightful situation.' In a guidebook of 1991 the author, we think rather unkindly, says of Banchory: 'this gifte-shoppe town has an air of net-curtain conservatism but there are signs that it is dragging itself into the twentieth century'.

The twentieth century saw a most dramatic change in Banchory. Just over a century ago it was a rural village, with a burgh population of 1,400 in 1891. The exploitation of North Sea oil and the changes it brought in its wake has made Banchory a dormitory town for Aberdeen, and in the 2001 census the urban population (now spread out beyond the former burgh boundaries) had risen to 6,034. There seems no end to this increase, and as we enter the twenty-first century the popularity of Banchory is assured. It is ideally situated 18 miles from a major city, with magnificent scenery and places of interest all around.

An aerial view of Banchory in the early 1930s with only a few granite-built houses on Ramsay Road. Many familiar buildings can be identified, such as the West Church, still one of the landmarks of Banchory's High Street. This was originally the Free Church and had its origins in the Disruption of 1843. The first Free Church building was at Loanhead (on Station Road at the corner of Raemoir Road). In September 1880 the present church was opened for worship and the old building, which stood in front of what was originally the Free Church School (later the Station Hotel and then the Kerloch Hotel before its recent conversion into flats), was levelled.

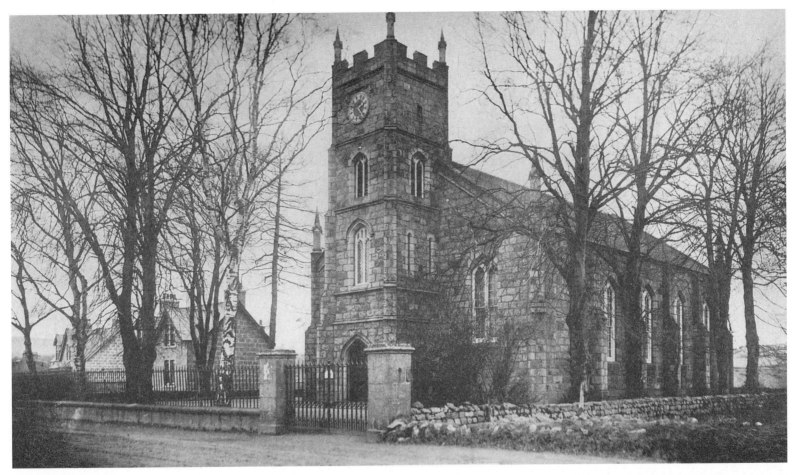

The Parish Church (East Parish Church since 1929) was built on this site in 1824-1825 using stones from the previous church which had been situated in the present kirkyard and had proved too small for the growing congregation. Between 1928 and 1930 the church was beautifully restored, with the addition of an apse and chancel, together with a vestry and choir room. This helped to remedy comments made nearly a century earlier by the Reverend William Anderson in the Statistical Account of 1842 when he described the church as: 'a plain substantial building in the Gothic style, sufficiently neat and commodious within, but defective in having the tower in front too low, and in having neither a vestry nor porches behind'. A small bronze handbell (dating from about 900), discovered during excavations of the glebe lands in 1863, now hangs within the church. This is undoubtedly the handbell which represented Ternan's legendary 'Ronnecht' (or Songster) during the medieval period.

Railway Station, Banchory

The Deeside Railway Company line from Aberdeen, originally proposed in 1845, reached Banchory in 1853 and the line opened on 8 September that year. It was extended to Ballater in 1866 and in 1876 was absorbed by the Great North of Scotland Railway (GNSR). In 1923 it became part of the London and North Eastern Railway before being absorbed by British Railways in 1948. The Beeching Report sealed the line's fate, and despite many local petitions passenger services were withdrawn on 26 February 1966 and the last goods service passed through Banchory in July of the same year. This picture, with a train proceeding to Ballater to the west, shows the extent of the station. It was unusual in being lit by acetylene gas right up until the time it closed. The gas was made in a small building (on the extreme right of picture), outside which a heap of white, spent carbide accumulated. The two cars and the people in the foreground have been crudely added to the picture to make it more interesting.

Banchory Station was reconstructed in 1902 with improvements including wider platforms and a covered footbridge. Writing in *A Dictionary of Deeside* in 1899, James Coutts described it as 'a station which is neither well built nor well situated, being placed at the eastern outskirts close to the churchyard, as if designed for nearness to the dead rather than the living'. One of the acetylene gas lamps is visible, as is the River Dee which runs very close to the line on the right. A housing estate now occupies the site of the station, which was demolished in 1970. Only the engine sheds remain.

G.N.S.R. No. 92 at Banchory Station.

GNSR locomotive class R 0-4-4T No. 92, photographed at Banchory Station. This was one of a batch of nine locomotives built by Neilson and Co. of Glasgow in 1893 for use on the Aberdeen suburban services (known locally as the 'subbies'). They were normally used on the Deeside line to Dyce and Culter, but occasionally worked to Banchory where at one time an engine of this class was shedded. This locomotive subsequently became LNER no. 6892 of class G10, and was scrapped in 1939.

In addition to the railway, buses provided a vital public transport service on Deeside. Strachan of Ballater was a familiar name from the 1920s until 1965 when they were taken over by the giant Alexander organisation. They served both the north Deeside route – between Aberdeen and Braemar via Banchory and Ballater – and the south Deeside route via Ballogie. This is one of Strachan's early Lancia buses, built in the mid-1920s and finished in the red livery carried by the fleet for forty years. It was photographed when new outside the works where it was built in North Acton, London.

The south side of the High Street decorated for Coronation Day 1902. Edward VII succeeded to the throne on the death of Queen Victoria on 22 January 1901, but because of illness his coronation was postponed until 9 August 1902. The following month he and Queen Alexandra cruised round the west coast of Scotland on the Royal Yacht, landing at Invergordon before heading for Aberdeen and onward to Balmoral on the Royal Train.

High Street, Banchory

D'Agostino's brings back fond memories both for locals and countless thousands of visitors to Banchory. Famed for its ice-cream, no visit to the town was ever complete without buying a 'slider' (ice-cream wafer) or cone there. This picture of the original shop shows Lorenzo D'Agostino standing at the door with one of his assistants. In 1924 D'Agostino's moved next door to the premises of Tavendale & Co. and A. Abernethy (now occupied by the Royal Bank of Scotland). Many will recall the tiled floor and the metal tables and chairs. It was a sad day when the shop closed its doors for business in the early 1970s.

MILL OF HIRN, BANCHORY.
W.J.J. COPYRIGHT.

A memorial tablet to James Scott Skinner, 'The Strathspey King', is set into the wall at the east end of the High Street opposite the top of Dee Street. Scott Skinner was born in a house near that spot in 1843. He later became a celebrated violinist and composer of Scottish reels and strathspeys. One of his most popular compositions – a strathspey, *The Miller o' Hirn* – perpetuates the name of this well-known mill which lies about four miles north-east of the village. Skinner wrote about the tune thus: 'it was amongst my early efforts, but, according to competent judges, it is one of my best. The old miller of Hirn, John Johnston by name, and my grandfather were married to sisters, and as a boy both the miller and the mill were objects of great veneration to me. Many a visit I paid to the mill, and later in life the feelings it had generated returned clamouring for expression on the lined sheet.' Scott Skinner died at Aberdeen in 1927. The mill continued to be worked until 1977 by Mr Norman Duncan, the farmer, who used it for corn dressing and hashing and bruising. It is now a private house.

The High Street at the beginning of the twentieth century. Gas for the street lights was manufactured at works in Bridge Street (often referred to as Gas Street). The lantern at the far right-hand edge of the picture belonged to Banchory post office, situated next door to Alexander Lunan's chemist's shop, with its mortar and pestle above the door. The water hydrant on the pavement beside the street light incorporates a rest for the pail. When an improved water supply to Banchory was provided in 1887 pillar fountains were installed in various parts of the town. At that time only the affluent could afford to have water piped into their houses.

HIGH STREET, BANCHORY.

This picture was taken about fifty years after the previous one and shows just how much the High Street changed in the intervening period. Gas lamps were replaced by electric lighting in 1932, and the trees at the top of Dee Street made way for Russell's shop. The shops on the north side of the street have all changed ownership and include J. M. Cook, grocer; the electricity office and showroom; George A. Hatt, chemist and druggist; Disney Cran (with a sign reading 'Your Murphy Dealers' above the door); and Durward's shoe shop. The post office has moved to the south side of the street. The railway bridge, just visible in the distance, was removed after the Deeside railway ceased operating in 1966.

14

The Burnett Arms Hotel was once a coaching inn. The crest above the door is a bit of a mystery – without doubt it shows the arms of William IV and his spouse Princess Adelaide, but quite why these arms should be displayed is unknown. The hotel does, however, have royal connections. On Wednesday 20 September 1854 *The Scotsman* reported that Queen Victoria, Prince Albert and the royal children visited the refreshment rooms on their annual journey to Balmoral, where 'luncheon was served in very elegant style by Mr Grant [of the Burnett Arms Inn]'.

The private taxi (left) belonging to the Burnett Arms collected passengers from the railway station and took them into Banchory. The low wall fronts The Banchory Coffee House and Reading Rooms, and further along cars sit outside Claud Hamilton's Garage.

HIGH STREET, BANCHORY.

A.2988.

Looking east along the High Street in about 1938. The 'baby' Austin is sitting outside the post office, beyond which is Robert Stewart, Ladies and Gents Hairdresser with barber's pole outside. Two doors beyond that lies D. Russell's grocer's shop, relocated from its old premises on the corner of Dee Street. The gentleman standing alongside his Humber car is none other than Charles McIntosh, Provost of Banchory from 1946 to 1948.

A.2546.   WAR MEMORIAL AND HIGH STREET, BANCHORY.

When this photograph was taken the premises (out of sight to the left) that the war memorial stood in front of were used as the burgh buildings. They had previously been the Reid and Burnett School, built in 1838 and closed in 1911. The site of Lamb's Garage had previously been occupied by Lamb's Boot Store. Alexander Lamb operated the first public petrol pumps on Deeside and also owned the first motor hearse. He was in business until the early 1950s, but the garage continued to trade under the name of Lamb until the mid 1980s. The town hall (right) was erected in 1872 and built under the aegis of the town council, a body first formed by John Watson in 1828. In 1888 it reconstituted itself into a corporate body under the name of The John Watson Guild, retaining control of the town hall. A major extension to the hall in the 1890s drove the Guild to near bankruptcy. By the 1960s it was still in their possession but was in a poor state. Ownership was transferred to the town council of the day, and it was refurbished and reopened in 1969.

This picture, dating from 1915, shows the dining room of the Banchory Hotel in the High Street, also known as Lewis's Hotel after the proprietor Mr Herbert Lewis. He may be the figure standing at the back of the room, waiting to serve an expectant group of cyclists or tourists. The hotel still flourishes today but is now called The Stag Hotel. Its By-Dee Inn is a popular bar.

The golf course was opened by Sir Thomas Burnett in July 1905. It was laid out on what was formerly the farm of Kinneskie, which became vacant in 1904 and was secured from the laird for conversion into a golf course by Provost Blacklaws and his influential committee. The Round Room (now the professional's shop) was the original clubhouse and the Doo'cot (marked on the first edition Ordnance Survey map) is another of the familiar landmarks of the course. The short 88 yard 16th hole is named after it. The leaflet on the course says of the hole: 'The Doo'cot is remembered as Banchory's signature hole. Although less than 100 yards long, pin point accuracy is required to find a green set above the ancient river bank. The resident Doos have witnessed many an unwary golfer humbled here.' In the late 1980s Paul Lawrie, Open Golf Champion in 1999, started his career as assistant professional at Banchory Golf Club.

Watson Street perpetuates the name of one of the early feuars of Banchory, John Watson, a farmer from Braemar and for some time tenant of the farm of Mills of Drum. The development of Banchory was to a great extent due to the vision of Watson – he devoted his energies so that in time it should become 'the most beautiful, populous and important place on Deeside'. He founded a town council, which all village residents were eligible to be members of on payment of an entrance fee of 2/6 (and thereafter an annual payment of 1/-). He gifted a piece of land around the public well behind the Burnett Arms Hotel 'to be embellished and laid out for the public weal'. This is part of what is now Watson Street (previously Bath Street). In 1847 the council's funds were used to welcome Queen Victoria on her first visit to Deeside, and the body later provided gas lighting for the village as well as setting up a Coal Fund in 1879. When Banchory became a Police Burgh in 1885 the old town council had to give up some of its powers and in 1888 reconstituted itself as The John Watson Guild. To this day it still looks after the needy in Banchory, and while no longer supplying coal it helps with their electricity bills.

Climbing up Mount Street (formerly Chapel Brae) one reaches the viewpoint known as Sunset Seat. There are excellent views to the south and west and of the hills of Kerloch, Scolty and Morven. The gentleman is looking east, possibly contemplating just how captivating the scenery is around Banchory and has been identified as John Lamb of Lamb's Shoe Shop which was on the High Street in Banchory.

TOR-NA- COILLE HOTEL, BANCHORY

E 04040

The imposing mansion of Tor-na-Coille on the outskirts of Banchory was built in 1873 at a cost of £1,000. It was to become one of Royal Deeside's best appointed hotels and still retains the Victorian elegance which, over the years, has attracted members of European royal families (and, apparently, Hollywood legend Charlie Chaplin). A souvenir and tariff booklet from the 1930s lists the hotel's charges, which include single rooms from 8 shillings per night, doubles from 14 shillings, with an extra daily charge of 2 shillings for a fire in the evening.

Nordrach-on-Dee was the first commercial sanatorium to be established in Scotland. It was the idea of Dr David Lawson of Banchory, who did much early work in the study of tuberculosis. He modelled the sanatorium on a similar establishment he had visited at Nordrach in the Black Forest. It was opened in 1900 and originally provided treatment for eighty patients, attracting people from throughout Britain in the early years. One distinguished resident was W. Somerset Maugham who was a TB sufferer and is reputed to have written several of his short stories during his stay. Certainly his story *Sanatorium* is based on his experiences at Nordrach-on-Dee. The sanatorium flourished until 1928 and then lay empty until it was bought in 1934 and reopened the following year as the Glen o' Dee Hotel. During the Second World War it was taken over by the army and housed men of various Scottish Regiments. In 1945 the Red Cross purchased the building for the care and treatment of ex-servicemen and women suffering from pulmonary tuberculosis, and after conversion it was opened in December 1948. The Red Cross gifted the building to the National Health Service in 1955 and it became a convalescent home. It is now closed and planning permission has been granted to convert the building into flats.

J. Hume Barry conducted his photography business from this shop on Dee Street from 1928 until 1947. Bellfield House, in the background, was the home of Deeside's first family doctor, Francis Adams. He had a practice in Banchory from 1815 until his death in 1861. Adams was a classical scholar as well as a doctor and married the only daughter of William Shaw, the first feuar in Banchory, through whom he acquired Bellfield. A monument to Adams' memory was erected in the south-west corner of the property. Bellfield is now a Church of Scotland Eventide Home.

Banchory Lodge was originally a coaching inn called Coble Heugh on the old Deeside Road. Before the bridge was built over the Dee in 1798 the ferry crossed the river at this point. In the late eighteenth century the house was restored and enlarged by General William Burnett, whose memory is commemorated by the tower on Scolty. On his death in 1839 the house passed to his grandnephew William Burnett Ramsay. A granite fountain erected to his memory stands on Station Road opposite Arbeadie Road, at what was once one of the entrances to the estate. Following the sale of the estate Banchory Lodge became the highly regarded hotel which it is today.

BOATING ON THE DEE AT BANCHORY

Boating on the River Dee could be hazardous in the nineteenth century when logs, tied together to form rafts, were floated down the river to the sawmills. This couple appear to have decided to come ashore close to Banchory Lodge. The Bridge of Dee is visible in the distance. The river has always played a significant part in the life of Banchory, and whilst traditionally famed for its salmon and trout fishing, kayaks and canoes are now a regular sight.

Bridge of Dee, Banchory.

66679, JV.

The first Bridge of Dee was built by public subscription in 1798 to replace the long-established ferry service at Coble Heugh at the junction with the River Feugh, where the Banchory Lodge Hotel stands. After the 1829 'muckle spate' an iron truss arch replaced the wooden arch, which had fallen into disrepair. This lasted until the start of the twentieth century when it was replaced by a further cast iron central structure. By the 1970s this had become dangerous, so a temporary Bailey bridge was installed until the present concrete arch was completed in 1985.

BLACKHALL CASTLE BANCHORY

The Blackhall estate was originally the home of the ancient Russell family, but in the early nineteenth century was taken over by Mr Archibald Farquharson of Finzean, MP, and subsequently by Col. John Campbell who started work on the castle. It was completed in the 1880s by James T. Hay, who had purchased the estate. Blackhall suffered serious deforestation in both World Wars and during the Second World War the castle housed St Margaret's School for Girls from Aberdeen. It was demolished in 1946 and its contents disposed of. The only item of furniture known to be held locally is a bracket clock displayed in the Banchory Museum.

One of the reasons for building the Bridge of Dee was to provide a link with the road that led to the gates of the Blackhall estate. The entrance to the estate (left) and the two mile drive is all that remains of Blackhall Castle now. The gate was originally surmounted by the figure of a goat, crest of the Russell family, with the motto *Che sara sara* ('What will be will be').

Crathes Castle, Banchory

Crathes Castle, situated three miles east of Banchory on land originally given by Robert the Bruce to Alexander de Burnard in 1323, is the traditional home of the Burnett family, lairds of Leys. The present castle, recognised as a fine example of Scottish Gothic architecture, was constructed in the second half of the sixteenth century. It was given to the National Trust for Scotland in 1951 by the thirteenth Baronet, Sir James Burnett. The internal rooms of the castle are well preserved and the plaster and painted ceilings are particularly fine. Alexander de Burnard's famous jewelled ivory hunting horn, given to him by Robert the Bruce, hangs in the Great Hall. The castle gardens are justly renowned with a splendid collection of British and foreign shrubs and plants, and the massive yew hedges which date from 1702.

Sir James Burnett and his wife Sybil, possibly photographed shortly after their marriage in July 1913, outside the Queen Anne wing of Crathes Castle. The wing was destroyed by fire in 1966 and has now been partly rebuilt. When closed, the old yett gate (left) made the castle virtually impregnable. The upper coat of arms above the gate (only partially visible) is that of Alexander Burnett and his wife Janet Hamilton, who began the building of the castle in 1553. The lower coat of arms, dated 1596 (the year that the castle was completed), is of their great-grandson Alexander and his wife Katherine Gordon. The arms to the left of the Queen Anne entrance are those of the first Baronet, Sir Thomas, and his second wife Jean Moncrieffe, and were brought from Muchalls Castle which was built by the Burnetts early in the seventeenth century.

THE OLD TOLL- BRIDGE OF FEUGH (IN BYGONE DAYS)

E04066

The Old Toll House at the Bridge of Feugh is one of the most photographed sights in Deeside and dates from 1790, when the bridge was built. Its design is unique among the toll houses of Deeside. A hundred years ago it was the home of John Moir, a blind shopkeeper and local poet. Some of his poetry was collected in *Feugh Spray*, published in 1898, and *Spray, Feugh Spray* (1903). The blackboard outside Moir's shop was covered with rhyming advertisements, and in this photograph the poem is on the subject of the Bonfire of Tilquhillie. The following short rhyme is an example of the service he provided to the local community via his blackboard:

A Wether Hog has stray'd away
If anyone find it today
Miss Malcolm will the same repay.

A.2989.   AT THE BRIG O' FEUGH, BANCHORY.

The Bridge of Feugh was a favourite spot for cyclists and tourists who could view the Falls of Feugh and hopefully see salmon leaping the cascading waters on their way to the spawning grounds further up the river. Little has changed over the years except that there is now an unattractive iron viewing platform for pedestrians.

Mr. A. Bowman diving
from Bridge of Feugh
Banchory.

In the early 1900s tourists could watch not only the salmon leaping but also Mr A. Bowman, who would regularly dive from the bridge into the pool on the north side for 'monetary reward' from the spectators. There is no record that he ever failed in his daring exploits!

Bridge of Feugh, Banchory (with River in Flood)

The River Feugh can quickly turn into a dramatic torrent of water when it is swollen by rainfall on the Mounth. On 3 and 4 August 1829 the Muckle Spate flooded the Old Toll House and the River Dee in Banchory rose to 27 feet above normal level. The Statistical Account of 1842 gives a vivid description of the bridge and river: 'A bridge of two principal arches is thrown over the stream, just below the fall; and few spots in the parish exhibit a more striking view than the alpine scenery of this place, especially when the Feugh, swollen by rain, fills the whole channel with a thundering noise, and foaming waters, [and] sweeps through the arches into the whirlpool below.'

Tilquhillie Castle Banchory

Tilquhillie Castle, (pronounced Tilwhillie and often spelled in this way in old documents), lies two miles south of Banchory. The name may come from the Gaelic, *tulach-choille* which means hillock of the wood. The lands of Tilquhillie originally belonged to the Abbey of Arbroath but in the late fifteenth century became the seat of the Douglas family through marriage. The castle was built in 1576 as a Z plan fortified house and commanded the Mounth route to the crossing of the Dee at Banchory. The Douglas family had many distinguished members and in the seventeenth century the brothers Archibald and Robert Douglas both received knighthoods from Charles I for bravery. By coincidence two ancient families whose residences (Crathes and Tilquhillie) are in view of each other on opposite sides of the Dee have each given a prelate – Bishop Burnett in the seventeenth century and Bishop Douglas in the eighteenth century – to the same see, Salisbury, in the English Church. For many years the castle, which has recently been restored, was lived in by the tenant of the farm which surrounds it.

This postcard is entitled 'The Banchory children's excursion to Aberdeen Beach'. The residents of Aberdeen have traditionally visited Banchory for outings at weekends and on holidays – indeed as many as 5,000 visitors are reputed to have come on one local holiday. However, the children of Banchory have always enjoyed travelling east for the pleasures of the sea, sand and other entertainments at Aberdeen beach. Now no more, the Beach Baths, in the background, were popular with visitors when the waters of the North Sea were too cold for swimming.

"The Royal Train," Banchory

This photograph of the Royal Train passing through the outskirts of Banchory on its way to Ballater, with Scolty Hill in the background, was probably taken in the 1920s in the early days of LNER. The first royal train left Banchory Station on 11 October 1853 with Queen Victoria's mother, the Duchess of Kent, on board. Two days later Queen Victoria with Prince Albert and their children also left amid great excitement. For the next 112 years the royal train was regularly seen carrying members of the British and foreign royal families between Aberdeen and Ballater. The train was always surrounded by strict security, especially at level crossings and points, and was headed by a pair of locomotives with other engines under steam at strategic junctions. The last royal train travelled through Banchory from Ballater on 15 October 1965.

THIS IS A REAL PHOTO

Inchmarlo House stands about a mile west of Banchory. During the seventeenth century the lands of Inchmarlo were acquired by the Douglas family, lairds of nearby Tilquhillie. In 1812 the estate passed into the hands of Walter Davidson, whose grandson George L. O. Davidson brought fame to Inchmarlo with his aeronautical experiments. Both the Douglases and the Davidsons were responsible for the planting of the magnificent woodlands. Little wonder that Queen Victoria would order her coach to be driven through the Inchmarlo estate on her way to and from Balmoral. The estate was acquired in 1983 by Skene Enterprises and has been developed as a nursing home and retirement complex.

The Aberdeen Waterworks at Invercannie, some 23 miles from Aberdeen, were opened by Queen Victoria on 16 October 1866. In his book *Deeside*, written in 1900, Alex McConnachie states that '6 million gallons of water are daily diverted from the Dee at a point 224 feet above sea level. The water is conveyed through a tunnel to a reservoir at Invercannie. Here there is storage for 10 million gallons.' Since opening the waterworks have been extended, and in the 1920s an agreement was reached with Aberdeen Corporation which allowed Banchory to receive a supply from the Invercannie to Aberdeen aqueduct.

The prominent building in the background is the Auction Mart which operated once a week and it was from there that Banchory butchers and many others bought their supplies. It stood on the north-west corner of the Market Stance, opposite the slaughter house. The Deeside Agricultural Association has been in existence since at least 1820, and it was here at the Market Stance opposite the Silverbank Sawmill that its show was held prior to 1913. The show, always held on the last Saturday of July, was then moved to Bellfield and later to its present venue, the King George V Park. The Third Statistical Account of the County of Kincardine records that in 1820 the first prize for stock shown was £5.5.0d whereas in 1950 the highest prize was no more than £1, although the expenses of the exhibitors must have increased tenfold!

Harvest time on Deeside was traditionally a very important time, and all the family had to assist. The crop was cut by hand (note the scythe) and then the stooks set up to dry. An 1879 entry in the log for the Central School (later to become Banchory Academy) reads: 'Friday August 15th – Gave out Summer Holidays for six weeks – Work to commence again on Wednesday 1st October'. How very sensible to arrange the holidays to suit work on the farm. It was customary to have a holiday to mark Harvest Thanksgiving, held when all the crops were safely gathered in. In 1879 this was not held until Wednesday 3 December – the exceptionally late harvest caused perhaps by bad weather.

HARVEST TIME ON DEESIDE, A STUDY NEAR BANCHORY.

E04056

The location is Woodend Farm, Crathes, in a field adjacent to the Ley Brae and the date around the turn of the century. The man on the binder is David Murray and the other his son Robert. Life on the farm has undergone tremendous changes in the last hundred years, and much of the romance has gone from the harvest fields with the development of mechanisation. There is now little need to dig for potatoes, once a laborious job for a man and his graip, and the combine harvester has replaced horses pulling the binder.

44

A LAVENDER FIELD NEAR BANCHORY OF THE "DEE VALLEY" PERFUME WORKS

One of Banchory's more unusual light industries was the cultivation and distillation of lavender and the manufacture of lavender water. The founder of this small operation was Mr A. R. Inkster, who had a chemist's business in the town. He conceived the idea of growing lavender in the light sandy soil of Deeside and formed a company, Ingasetter Limited, to develop the process commercially. The lavender was grown in a field on the western outskirts of Banchory. A small factory was built near New Banchory (on a site now occupied by a supermarket) and it was there that the distillation took place and the resultant Dee Lavender Water was manufactured. It sold all over the world, and was even to be found in Raffles Hotel in Singapore! An antique-style crystal flask filled with this fragrant lavender water was sent by the people of Crathie as a wedding gift to Princess Elizabeth in 1947.

The Third Statistical Account of the County of Kincardine records how sawmilling was one of Banchory's major industries. The firm of Messrs A. & G. Paterson Ltd. built a mill alongside the new railway line at Silverbank in 1854, and business was carried on there for more than a century. A sawmill still operates on the same site under the name James Cordiner & Son Ltd. Timber was originally floated down the river, and stones with iron rings for tying up the timber rafts can still be seen on the riverbank below the sawmills.

The bobbin mills belonging to James and John Low Brebner were closed down many years ago and the work transferred to King Street in Aberdeen. When it was closed it became a public house known as the Bobbin Mill. Mr C. Fraser's sawmill stood nearby, as did Duncan's Sawmill at Invercannie (this was originally three mills – a turning mill, meal mill and a sawmill). Duncan's mill was taken over by Mr J. S. Duthie for some years and in 1941 passed into the hands of Messrs Rosowsky and Blumstein who carried it on as a sawmill. Shortly after the Second World War, owing to the shortage of timber in the locality, the sawmill was forced to shut down.

Banchory Central School was built at Schoolhill in 1878, and Arbeadie, shown in the picture, lies half a mile to the north. These houses can still all be identified, although many have been altered. The fields have now made way for more housing, and the tranquil picture of sheep grazing has been lost for ever.